written by a
HEAVY HEART

M.S.Pearly

mspearlysm@gmail.com

ISBN: 9798352522721

To all my lovers;
thank you for the inspiration.

A typical heart is divided into four chambers
one more thing from school that no one remembers
I believe the body is a village
and I think of these chambers as
a house with a garden
a home
a home
you need to take care of
don't let everybody in
or you'll get hurt and robbed
don't lock yourself in
or you'll end up lonely.

My heart
is a house full of chaos, love and art
I grow flowers of smiles in the front yard
so that you won't suspect any pain in the backyard
and I keep my cold face like a dog to guard
because I can't keep kindness and interest apart.

he

you

me

For all these years
I kept my front door wide open
always hoping
for someone to arrive
who feels like home in my heart
he felt like that right from the start.

I'm never quite sure where to look at
I want to
watch how his lips move
measure his jaw
inspect his long lashes
it's impossible to find a place
to comfortably rest my eyes
I wanna see everything about him
everything at once.

When he's around
life feels simple
I'm ready to drown
in his damned dimples
he has the prettiest eyes
I've ever seen
forest green
easy to get lost in.

Every time I see him on the streets
I want to meet him under the sheets
I really want to get to know him
to find out what's so different about him
and why I want to please him.

He swallows
a sip of wine
while his eyes follow
my deep neckline
we talk slow
I stutter
because I didn't know
that his voice
can be as soft as butter.

Falling for him is as easy as breathing
but I'm falling for a boy with a mind
set on leaving
I just want to be something to him
because he's everything to me.

He smells like smoke
but I press my nose against his neck
as if he smells like flowers
skinny dip into his eyes
I think I love the way he lies.

I rather listen to him
reading the phone book
than anyone
reading my favorite book.

When I walk next to him
I always feel like dancing

but I never do.

My body feels swollen with desire
he burns inside me like a fire
I don't know how to be affectionate
with anyone
but with him
my body already seems to know
what to do.

I'm wearing silk
skin underneath
soft as milk
down to the sheet
where our bodies meet.

I can't care less
about the twinge of nervousness
while my words get lost between his lips
while I feel his hands on my hips
he spends the next seconds tearing off my clothes
pulling me close
with eager hands
and dirty plans.

I stare at his ceiling
while getting the feeling
that I've been abused
my body is bruised
I feel used
confused
cheap
he fell asleep
silently.
Does he want me to stay?
Does he wish me away?
How can he feel so far away
after kissing my toes
after removing all my clothes
after seeing spots no one else knows
after being so close?

I feel used
because of hands that touched and wanted
but didn't hold me.

9:34
I feel sore
he doesn't look at me
not the way he has before
more like I am now a whore
doesn't he want me anymore?
He eats bread and confidence for breakfast
I play with my necklace
suddenly he looks too tall
I stare at the wall
and eat nothing at all.

I kiss him goodbye
and can't stop crying
the whole way home.

He says he misses me
and that he wants to see me
and I'm the worst at saying *no*
especially to him
after all
it wasn't his fault
I didn't say no or stop
I didn't say anything at all
I'm just good at exaggerating
and bad at communicating.

The clouds above us
change their clothes
from white to orange to red to grey
I never know which words he'll say
we talk through the night
while watching the lake in the moonlight
and I force myself to forget my sore limbs
so I can remember the angelic way he swims.

Everyone likes him
that's what I thought
before I got to know him
but he calls himself a lot
and a lot of other ugly things
like untalented and plain
though he's very talented at playing on my heartstrings
and I'm pretty sure he's meant to wear wings
and he's running marathons through my brain
and he's the best at hiding his pain.

Everyone likes him
everyone
except one.

Let me love you
long and hard
open your heart
let me in
I wanna be closer than
skin to skin.

I want to write him love letters
and leave my scent on his sweaters
I want to create our travel bucket list
and feel his lips on my hand and wrist
I want us to play Romeo and Juliet
and him to come around when I'm upset
I often forget
that we're not in a relationship
we're just another silly situationship.

Don't we all just want to own a place
where we can fall asleep peacefully?

Flashbacks won't stop playing in my head
him in my bed
eyes closed
naked and exposed.

He leaves the room
and I feel empty.

Can you
come back
and fuck me
so I feel whole again?

I'm in love with his features
he could be descended from divine creatures
maybe his mother is an angel
he's got the ideal gonial angle
120 degrees
and I swear he has perfect knees
I just keep hearing myself saying please
and when he raises his hand - I freeze
and I'm not sure I am what he sees.

He really is beautiful.
But he makes me feel so ugly.

I would rather get burned
than take my fingers off his skin.

I stopped wearing caps
because he doesn't like them on girls
he buys me cute hats
and make-up and pearls.

He wants me to be the girl
with perfect hair
but I'm the girl who doesn't care
about the pictures when we kiss.

When I am with him
my limbs feel sore
I always sit near the door
I always look outside
feel numb inside
feel like crying
or dying.

I don't wanna be
all alone
but with him
loneliness is all I know
so maybe
just me
wouldn't be so lonely
maybe
it wouldn't be so hurtful
maybe
I wouldn't lie
awake all night
hoping he'll come back
all right.

I always call when I'm excited
he calls me when he's bored
I wouldn't change a thing about him
he says my legs are too short
I always call when I can't sleep
he calls me pretty
but never picks up the phone.

How is he able to hurt me
and tell me he loves me
just a minute later?

I'm losing my mind
while trying to figure out his.

Every time I force myself to ignore
the bad of us
I ignore
the part of me that was hurt
and every time I force myself to remember
his good parts only
it feels like I'm forgetting
a part of myself.

His love is like a dress
that's too tight
and to fit in
I need to lose weight
and watch my diet
and barely breath.

Just say you won't come back to me
and I will cope
but don't leave me drowning here in hope.

heavy heart

When the sun sets
it takes him four cigarettes
and three glasses of whiskey
to admit that he misses me.

My love,
are you that scared of love?

He often feels like a warm bed
impossible to leave
especially in the dark and cold nights
but his arms
are starting to feel like chains
and I miss so much of my life
while staring at the ceiling
scared to get up
and do something wrong.

I'd rather be there for him
than anywhere else for me.

I want to rip my heart out
leave it in his bed
so it stops feeling lonely in the nights
when he's busy seeing someone else.

I'm getting drunk
just to pass the time
I can't call him mine
and I keep texting him
to be the one on his mind
but he keeps ignoring my texts
as if he has suddenly gone blind.

He told me he misses me
and I told him I miss him
we were on the phone
and I should've known
that I'm just a flirt
that his name will hurt
because when he told me he misses me
and I told him I miss him
he was thinking about my face
and I was thinking about his embrace.

heavy heart

It's not only about keeping a promise
it's about wanting to keep it.

He slept with someone else.
Again.
And told me he was sorry.
Again.
And I forgave him.
Again.
And then we did the same things.
Cry.
Kiss.
Sex.
Sleep.
Eat.
Repeat.
But it doesn't feel the same.
It feels unfamiliar and bland.
He feels unfamiliar and bland.

Everything is too much
so why do I still want more?

Being loved by him
is like being loved by the sea
always being pulled back and forth
I'm almost drowning in his love
at high tide
but at low tide
he's pulling back quick
leaving me seasick.

Because of him
I keep telling myself
that I must undress
and always say yes
to feel loved.

It's autumn
we run away from the city
into the woods
swimming in a sea of leaves
he calls me pretty
and I feel like crying
picking up a colorful leaf
thinking
they look most beautiful while dying.

Will he ever look at me the way I look at him?
Will he ever wait for me the way I wait for him?
Will he ever
Will he ever
Will he ever love me back?

I struggle to look at food
just because he switched his mood
suddenly he smiles so sweet
but I feel like a piece of raw meat
muted
denuded.

I'm waiting for him to realize that
just because I'm willing to do
anything for him
doesn't mean he has to take
everything from me.

I guess sometimes
you shouldn't be close
to the person you love the most.

I bring the fabric of his hoodie
up to my nose
and for the first time
it hurts to breathe him in.

He treats me like clay
I think about him all day
he forgets foreplay and my birthday
but remembers all the words he needs to say
to make me want to stay
he always gets his way
I feel like clay.

I'm so tired of
being always too loud
and never enough
so tired of
being held by arms
that are just doing it
out of habit.

Sometimes
when he's near
I feel like a torn deer
other times
when he looks at me
I feel like a hungry coyote
either way
it doesn't feel good.

He left
and I'm scared that
I'll always fall asleep to the memories
of his fingers on my skin
I'm scared that
my heart will still drop
one year from now
when I get a message that isn't from him
I'm scared that
I'll never be able to stop talking
about a man that broke me
I'm scared that
I'll think of him on my wedding day
I'm scared that
I'll have children one day
and look at the last name on their birth certificate
and feel sad because it's not his
I'm scared that
my heart will never stop waiting for him.

heavy heart

Can't start healing
because every time he's leaving
he's stealing
another part of my heart.

I never tell him how badly I want him to stay
I never call and say
hey
I met a new distraction
searching for satisfaction
he buys me flowers
and I could stare at him for hours
I love his brown eyes
and that he never lies
it's just that he could give it all
but if you would ever call
I would be your only
and he would be left lonely.

The fire
he started in me
burned down everything
now I'm left with nothing.

He taught me that
how you feel about someone
and how someone makes you feel
are two very different things
because I think that he's charismatic and cute
but he makes me feel
stressed and sad.

He smiled at me today.
I hate him for that.
He smiled at me like he misses me
but I know he doesn't.
Does he even know the damage
one smile can do?
Clearly not.
Or maybe he just doesn't care.

Day by day
I gave parts of me away
gave him everything he required
everything he desired
because he's only twenty
his home shouldn't be empty
I removed the frost
around his heart
and made it soft
planted seeds full of love in his backyard
watched them grow
I'm glad that his home is full of love now.

Everything and everyone
around me is growing
but my garden is rotting
I'm rotting.

I saw him again today
I think that's the problem;
it's impossible to get him off my mind
if I still see him all the time
someone should've told me that you shouldn't fall
for someone you keep seeing everywhere
I really wanna move on but there he is;
again.

How should I move on
and forget him
and his stupid lips
when his heart is still
right next to mine?

We went on and off for a while
and it became hard for me to smile
so after he broke once again my heart
and asked me once again for a fresh start

I said no today.
It's his first time not getting his way
and my first time feeling relief
while watching him leave.

All along
I thought it all went wrong
because of too much love
I thought that was
why I would've starved myself to death for him
why I watered his plants and let my garden rot
why I gave him everything of me
without a second thought
but I didn't love him too much
I just don't love myself enough.

There's no such thing as too much love.

Letting him go
is realizing
I can't be
me
and
what he wants.

I choose me
because I chose him for way too long
and it started to feel very wrong.

I'll look after myself
and stay away from him
until my heart is done
waiting for him.

We lost touch
and I never felt
more lost
without his touch.

heavy heart

I think I was just a vacation home for him
which is fine
it just hurts
that he won't be forever mine.

A soft heart easily tears apart.
A soft heart is art.

I'm wearing all his insecurities
on me like accessories
that can't be removed
even though he already moved
to another village.

All I wanted
was to feel wanted.

I still want him to want
no one but me.

I wish
he wouldn't have said
I love you
because he often hurt me
before saying these three words
and now I always feel like
love has to hurt
and if it doesn't hurt
it cannot be love.

He fucked me up.

Why was I so scared of losing him?
Why was I so scared of losing someone
who never belonged with me?

I feel like a house
where no one lives
a house
not a home anymore
right now
I want no one to move in
no one but me
I somehow forgot
that it's my village.
My house.
My heart.
My home.

He's gone
and I won't forget him
he taught me how to swim
by throwing me in cold water
smiling while I almost drowned
but I didn't
even though I hit the ground.

I thought he left me with nothing
but I found parts of him
in my heart and home
that I can't throw out;
like furniture full of memories
of all the days
he made me smile in so many ways
when he took me out for dinner
and didn't expect me to be thinner
memories of all the nights
we didn't fight
when he loved me softly
and couldn't stop staring at me.

I think it's okay
that these parts of him stay
because finding peace
includes not forcing leftover love to leave.

A life without selflove
is like a garden without a single fruit tree
most people
people like me
grew up in a house full of love
with a garden full of trees and seeds
that their loved ones have planted
they can enjoy the sweet taste any time
and exchange fruits with others
but some people
people like him
grew up in a garden where no one
has planted a single tree
it's okay to take fruits from other gardens
I wanted him to take my fruits
so he could enjoy the taste
and plant the seeds in his own garden
and he did
but somewhere along the way
I forgot to look after my own garden
and watered his seeds only
he didn't care enough to remind me
so my garden began rotting
and I was left without a single fruit tree.
I became dependent on his garden to get love.

he

you

me

I'm not quite sure
when or where
you became a part of my heart
because you were already there
when I was busy healing
busy staring at the ceiling
busy not looking for someone new
busy not noticing you
because you were just a friend
and I was sure that love is a dead end
so I didn't care about your silly pick-up lines
or that you hugged me tightly multiple times.

When did *you* become a part of my heart?

You and me
we clicked immediately
when walking the same way
we stick together like clay
I laugh at everything you say
with you the sky doesn't look so grey
and I believe that everything's gonna be okay.

My heart hasn't healed
so I keep my mind as a shield
and convince me I want to be alone
which is why I put you in the friend zone.

But I do miss
having someone to miss.

You keep wandering around my heart
waiting for an open door
while I'm lying on the bathroom floor
staring at the ceiling
internal bleeding
feeling exposed
I keep every entrance closed
and my blinds shut
but you don't give up
you're still trying to call
but I'm only talking to the wall.

I'm not scared of love
that's not why I locked the doors
I'm not scared of being yours
I'm scared to be your only
just to be left lonely
I'm scared to go from being
your first and last text of the day
to someone you don't want to stay
I'm scared of watching love leave
to be the one left alone in grief
and I'm not even as scared of being someday a ghost
as I am of being *another almost*.

I don't wanna let you in
but being away from you feels like a sin
against my nature
you sweet creature.

I want to give you everything
but I gave everything to him
and he left with it.

To my surprise
I suddenly find it quite annoying
that you're enjoying
your time with a girl who isn't me
and I suddenly
am having a hard time
when I'm not constantly
hearing a silly pickup line.

My body burns with jealousy
as I keep on denying chemistry.

It always hurts
seeing your other half
being completed by someone else.

If I can't touch you
I want to touch what light leaves after it touches you
so I'm tracing your shadow with my hand
as if I am discovering new land
feeling this much was never the plan.

heavy heart

I'm stretched out in my bed
you're stretched out in my head.

I'm falling for you
soft and slow
like snow
not hard and fast
like in the past.

You're looking at me
with blue eyes full of admiration
and suddenly I feel the earth's rotation
and suddenly I'm quite busy feeling dizzy.

I never planned to feel
that much for you.

You're keeping my heavy heart
soft and kind
his words are on my mind
but your smile is on my heart.

Every time you complain that I'm too closed up
I wish you'd know
that he showed me everything about him
especially the ugly parts
and I still wanted him
but I showed him all my good parts
hiding the bad and ugly stuff
and he still didn't want me.

Why should I tell you anything
if anything won't be enough?

I'm scared that you'll see
parts of him in me
because I'm like him before he met me
I'm like a garden without a single tree
like a house locked and completely empty
to which I lost every single key
and you should know
that everything I am right now
is everything I never want you to be
so please don't love me.

heavy heart

You look at me with so much love
it makes me sick
because you look at me with love
I'm not able to give back.

You make me question
if I've been buried under my problems
maybe I've been planted in them
they are like water
help me grow
some plants need more time than others
and that's all right
all-natural
you make me feel natural
maybe I'll find my way to the surface.

When I am lonely
I want your arms only
because when I feel like I have no one
you make me feel like I have everyone.

You're laughing and living
like your existence didn't just
change my life forever and ever.

Can I call you mine?
When you look at me I feel like nine
like everything's fine
we're drinking wine
goosebumps dancing down my spine
you kinda struggle not to shine.

You have the gift of making
everything heavy easy.

When I lie next to you I feel the weight
of a love without an expiration date.

When I met you
I was closed
careful
cautious
considerate
you really did come blindly
your love creeps up on me silently.

You try to never complain
you always adapt
just like your parents taught you
that's why they are so proud of you
but love,
I'm not with you because you're easy
I'm with you because you're the only one
who makes me feel at home
so try me
go wild
make mistakes
and watch me smile while you do.

I'm not surprised that I adore you
I've always been the person standing in the corner
with arms crossed
getting lost
in beautiful things
like sunrises
flowers
smiles
the sound of rain
the moon
you've always been the person joking
running through the world with arms wide open
I'm not surprised that I adore you
you're the most beautiful thing
I've ever seen.

I shouldn't be surprised that you adore me
you love ugly things and how they look
(I'm the only one calling them ugly)
you love rats and a heartbreaking book
and the night with all its darkness
you love mess and having stress
and for some weird reason
you keep saying
that autumn is your favorite season;
the season when everything is decaying.
It was autumn and I was still in grief
when you gave me a colorful leaf
and said it for the first time:
I want you to be mine.

All I wanna be
is a place where you can fall asleep peacefully.

Somewhere along the way
my feelings for him got lost
like water in the sand
still there
but buried deep down
I never wanna dig them out again.

I call it nowhere
unless you're there.

I don't fit in anywhere
except your arms.

I always missed him the most
when I was alone
but I miss you the most
when everyone's around.

You changed me
without wanting to change me.

I always called him smart
for leaving me
but you call him crazy and blind
because in your mind
he's the devil
and I'm the angel.

His love hit me like a lightning
it was beautiful and frightening
with you, I found love waiting
hesitating
for something that didn't seems like much
like one word, one glance, one touch
one gap to slip in my heart
where love spread seeds like art
they stayed there unchanged for a season
but they were there for a reason
and in spring
staring at you became a thing
because without me knowing
the seeds started growing
and suddenly I started caring
and suddenly I started staring
and suddenly I was obsessed
and suddenly there is a flower in my chest
which scent messes with my head too much
it wasn't just one word, one glance, one touch.

I loved sleeping alone
before I knew the safety of your bed
you wake me up so soft
I forget the war in my head.

You look at my eyes
like there's the sun inside.

Stop talking
kiss me
I don't want to
hear those words
I want to
feel those words.

You hold my hand
the same way you did before
but nothing feels like before
because my lips taste like you
and your eyes taste like me.

We talk about things
I never thought about
I always wanted him to say my name
over and over again
because it felt good
but maybe I just craved my name
a part of myself
because I love listening to all your words and stories
and I crave every word that comes out of your mouth.

He started a war in my head
and you stop it
you hold me tight
whisper
everything's gonna be alright
and I believe you.

Being with you is like drinking an expresso
and looking at you is like listening to music
or covering myself with a blanket
or drinking warm milk
and touching your skin
is like touching silk.

Falling in love with you
feels like falling in love with the world.

You shine bright
brighter than any light
so I wonder, hun
did you swallow the sun?

I kiss you goodbye
and can't stop smiling
the whole way home.

You're like that one song
I never get tired of
I could listen to you
over and over
again.

To know you is to love you.

I've been missed
I've been kissed
but never like this.

I want to get lost in this world with you.

Every night I lie in bed
and think of you
with my eyes closed
and my mind open.

In the morning
when the sun peeks out
from behind the curtain
and finds my face
that's how it feels
when you look at me
like I'm sleeping
and you tickle my nose
and I squeeze my eyes
because I'm not used to life being that bright
you scare away the darkness
put a spot of light on me
and I feel like an animal
after hibernation
famished
thirsty
hungry for life.

You
look at me
and I blush
but I don't hate it
it's nice to be looked at
as if I am something special.

Discovering new land
while we shower
I take your hand
which is veined
like the petal of a flower
I'm going to drown in this tension
I always hated being in the center of attention
but I want to be your center of attention
I want to be yours.

You ask for permission to touch my body
and for the first time it feels like I don't belong to
everyone that wants me
it feels like this body only belongs to me
for the first time I feel valuable
and able to say no
which is why I say yes
so confident.

I wonder what it feels like to you
to touch hips that are way too wide
to touch everything I'm trying to hide
because when I touch my body
all I feel is fat
are you really turned on by *that*?

Seems like I can't look in the mirror for too long
without hearing his words
which are reminding me of all the reasons
why no one will ever truly love me.

They say love yourself before getting into a relationship
but I was so lost without you
I didn't even know how to start loving myself
being loved by you
while hating myself
is constantly worrying
about which parts to show you
just to find out
you love every single one
being loved by you
while hating myself
is standing in an empty house
surrounded by a rotten garden
while you hang pictures on the wall
while you fill the house with life
while you grow flowers
in the darkest part of my heart.

When I look at your face
your eyes turn into a maze
and I don't want to find
the one way out.

You simply just look at me
and my heart gets so heavy
I'm afraid my legs won't
hold me much longer.

We stare at each other
I start to smile
and you whisper *what* after a while
I want to say
everything
but I shake my head
and answer *nothing* instead.

Because e*verything* sounds like a lot.

I'm touching
all the places where your lips have been
and all the places I want your lips to be
you taught me
how to touch me softly
so when I am alone
I can love myself on my own.

Kissing you is incredible and intimate
like sex or lying naked in bed together
being kissed by you is ...

I have no words for that.

You spend the whole night undressing me with your eyes
before my last piece of clothing falls on the floor
you're never rushing
your eyes are blushing
and I feel like a soldier going to battle
without armour
my knees are shaking and I move to the bed
lying naked on the battlefield
ready to be defeated.

It's so much more intimate
when nothing is perfect.

How come my biggest fears
turn into my biggest adventures
when I'm around you?
We can't tell our limbs apart
and I hate being trapped
but never with you
I would rob a whole bank
if prisons were made out of you.

You kiss every inch of my body
and make sure I'm eating
and my heart gets heavy
because no one has ever cared for me that way
I'm not quite sure I like the feeling
it's sort of like I can't breathe.

Hours turn into seconds with you
and seconds into hours without you
like time only passes
when I spend it with you.

I lost my mind
somewhere between your lips and feet
your body is meant to be desired
I know all your insecurities by heart
I'll turn them into art
your mind is meant to be admired.

Dazed
and amazed
by your gaze
eyes like a maze
hands hug my face
love is like an embrace.

I wish I had more hands and eyes
so I could see and touch more of you
at the same moment.

Sometimes you just look at me
or walk through the room
or smile at the red sky
and I find myself
needing you
again
and
again
and
again.

Almost as lovely as touching you
is knowing that I always could.

heavy heart

You smile
scenes from last night are playing in your eyes
and I can't look away.

I want to make you fall apart
and watch your legs tremble
like a leaf in the wind.

The more
I have of you
the more I want you.

It took me some time to realize that I love you
because your love doesn't feel like storms colliding
it didn't hit me like lightning
when you're mad at me
I still eat
and I'm not constantly worrying if you might cheat
you help cleaning up my mess
and never ask me to wear a dress
my heart gets heavy when we kiss
and I didn't expect love to feel like this
I thought it was about chasing highs and butterflies
but you proved me otherwise
because I love it when we cry
and the fact that you never lie
you never make me bleed
it's your healing love I need.

Your hands move
soft and slow
like snow
falling from the sky
you look me in the eye
while I feel them on my thigh.

I kiss you
and you kiss me
I run my fingers through your hair
and it feels like I just got off a rollercoaster ride.

Sex with you almost feels
too good
too soft
too much of everything
I've always wanted.

The sun burns away the spring
you smell like sex and summer
and I smell like you.

Skin on skin
we are going to do it face-to-face
which is so intimate that
my legs are already shaking
I love the sounds you're making.

Everything feels plastic without you
everything won't make any sense
when you're away from me.

You make me hate distance
make me love closeness
let's be coexistence
and forget the rest.

He taught me that love hurts.
You're teaching me that love heals.

You undressed my soul and heart first
before you undressed my body.

You make me understand what sex is about
before you
it was nice
it felt good
sometimes not so good
but you don't undress me
to satisfy your lust
you undress me to be closer to me
to my heart and soul
you have sex with me
to be as close to me
as you physically could
and then you watch me
you watch me the whole time
watch me fall apart
underneath you
watch me let go
of every doubt
watch me watching you
you don't say a word
but I can read
I love you
from your eyes.

You make me feel beautiful.

You say my name so softly
like you're reading a poem
or saying a compliment
or saying I love you.

I wrap my arms around you
and never in my life have I held
something so precious
it feels like hugging the whole world
maybe because you are my whole world.

We kiss
and I want to melt into you
to never have to leave you.

When I walk next to you
I always feel like dancing
so I sometimes do.

You laugh
eyes closed
open heart
and I fall in love
all over again.

You really are beautiful.

I love that
when we go to sleep
you put your phone on mine
and your ring on the bedside table
around mine
before you wrap your arms around me
everything of you is hugging everything of me.

Hold me tight
I wanna smell like you.

Sometimes I wish
we could fall down the horizon together.

Your love is like a jumper
it keeps me warm
it feels comfortable
it's a bit too wide
but there's plenty of room
for me to grow into.

You show me
everything I am
and everything I could be
you show me what I can't see
and make me a person
I didn't know I wanted to be.

I crave your softness
more than your hardness.

It's one thing to arouse a man
quite another to make him feel at ease
to put him down on his knees
just by thinking *please*
love them tender
and they will surrender.

I was a mess
a mental confusion
you make me feel
like a solution
I learned that skies are grey
so we can stay in bed all-day
that there is pain
so we can dance with tears in the rain
I always smile
when time flies fast
because every minute with you
is better than the last.

The thing I like most about you is that
you never tried to change me
you take me for who I am
with all my stupid problems
and the chaos inside my head
you never tried to fix me
I've never felt like a lost cause around you
not once
you make me feel so whole
and in the end
that is what fixed me.

I said I never wanted to fall again this deep
but with you, my pain falls asleep
with you, I feel complete.

You burn inside me like a fever
that won't break
you sweet creature,
why does my body always call out for you?

Your love feels like the warmest embrace
I found myself caressing my face
I found myself following the memories of your fingers
I found myself on the spot where your mouth always lingers
I found myself talking to you about everything
I found myself.

If you would come
an inch closer
you could hear the beat of my heart
singing over and over
I'm yours, I'm yours, I'm yours.

I'm not saying
I love you
to hear it back
I'm saying it
to remind you.

I would've burned down the world for him
but with you
I want to build another.

Even the moon can't get enough of you
I watch him follow you through the room
and when he can't handle your beauty anymore
he hides in the morning light
I wonder if he's jealous of the sun
when it's her turn to touch you
because I'm jealous of everyone and everything
that touches you.

I always thought true love is about being selfless
but I realized I would catch a bullet for you
because I'd rather die than live without you
so maybe true love is about being selfish
it makes you think about yourself
I want to watch after you
and keep you safe
because I cannot stand the thought of losing you.

Before you
I always felt so different
like I belonged nowhere
but with you, it feels like
something fell apart
thousands of years ago
parts of the universe broke in two
and they are in me and you
and when we are together
these parts tell me that
we're meant to be forever
whatever we are
we're meant to be together.

I never understood what life is about
until I tried to imagine my life without you.

When I imagine my future
I see a bed that smells like you
on which you can find my hair
I see kids with your eyes
and my nose.

How stupid of me to think
that I wouldn't get over him.

My home is
wrapped in skin only
it's the place I go
when I feel lonely
my home is
you.

I don't mind that you've been here with her
I'm not your first love
I'm not your first kiss
but please let me be your last kiss
let me be forever the one you miss
let me be your last love.

You're planting all these flowers
you leave my cheeks painted for hours
I call my heart ours.

I want to be your forever view
in the morning when the sun comes through
I want to be like glue for you
a home for us two
a house where my friends love to stay
a house where someday
our children's friends want to
come to.

You see
the transition between chapter
you and *me*
is clean
maybe that's what love means;
when you can no longer tell apart
which part
of the heart
belongs to you and which part to me.

Don't let your mind
be the prison of your heart.

Love should be like comfortable clothing.
Clothes are meant to fit us
not the other way around.
Sometimes it just doesn't fit
and that's not your fault
it doesn't mean you should change.
Other times it fits
and when you grow they grow with you
or when you grow you outgrow them.
It's okay
don't worry
you'll find the perfect fit.

Choosing you
means
choosing me
means
loving me
means
peace for me.

he

you

me

written by a
SOFT SOUL

I'm still learning
how to miss someone
without wanting them back
how to cherish the memories
without clinging to the past
how to appreciate the lessons
without regretting the mistakes
how to love someone
without needing them to stay
I'm still learning.

M.S.Pearly

Sometimes I look up at the sky
and wonder if maybe
I'm meant
for a different galaxy,
one where softness
isn't punished with pain.

We are all just fragments of the universe,
searching for a place to belong.

Your tragedy is not feeling too deep.
Your tragedy is thinking everyone does.

Made in the USA
Las Vegas, NV
11 December 2023